How to Be: NORTH DAKOTA

How to Be: NORTH DAKOTA
A Guide to the Plains

by Abe Sauer

with drawings by Amy Jean Porter

IlaDane Press

Published by
IlaDane Press
3808 37th Ave. South
Minneapolis, MN 55406
www . benorthdakota . com

First Printing: November 2011

ISBN-13: 978-0615553641 (How to Be: NORTH DAKOTA)

ISBN-10: 0615553648

Cover drawing by Amy Jean Porter.

Printed in the U.S.A.

Chapter Index

How to Be: NORTH DAKOTA

Congratulations!

You have taken the first step to being North Dakotan. Just by possessing this guide, you are following in the footsteps of thousands of pioneers and homesteaders who came to create, embody, and eventually try and escape what it means to be North Dakotan. Of course, their footsteps were actual footsteps, millions of them, planted in a frozen hellscape that was hardly the promised land the railroad pamphlets made it out to be.

As the owner of this guide you likely came by it one of six ways:

1) You fled North Dakota at an early age to "have a life" but remain nostalgic about the place all your current friends and acquaintances mock and deride as an expansive backwater where the film "Fargo" came from.

How to Be: NORTH DAKOTA

2) You are temporarily assigned here by the Air Force. Many who are stationed in North Dakota, even for only a short time, find that the state leaves its mark. For this, there is lotion.

3) You have a friend or relative in North Dakota with a sense of humor who knows or has met the author of the book and, possibly, was made to feel some degree of pressure about how this book is an excellent baby shower, Christmas, birthday, Passover, Kwanza, or Martin Luther King Jr. Day present for those living far away. Anyway, Mazel Tov! Or as they say in North Dakota, mowzeltaaaf!

4) You find having a guide to becoming a North Dakotan an amusing and "ironic" addition to your bookshelf because you are condescending. Incidentally, how is life in Minneapolis?

5) You acquired it used, the book having received the endorsement of whoever left it in the stall in the Fargo Dome where you're now sitting.

6) You actually are North Dakotan. And because you want your child's values and character to represent those of the great state of North Dakota you will be returning this book for a full refund tomorrow.

No matter which of these wild generalizations best exactly fits your situation, this guide to becoming North Dakotan has been designed to provide every individual with a personalized program so that all who use it will end up exactly the same, true North Dakotans, Yes, even those too selfish or vitamin-D deficient to actually live there.

A Guide to the Plains

After completing this book, you will know the difference between an outhouse and an ice fishing house is that one is a small shack over a hole in which a man sits and waits, straining. The other is a small shack in which a man poops. You will be able to "teach the controversy" about Teddy Roosevelt's North Dakotaness. You will finally be able to grow a mustache.

Yes, even women.

In the exhausting and demanding days and weeks and months and years and decades ahead, all of which are sure to try your very soul, always remember that no matter how poor a North Dakotan you or your child turn out to be, you are all already better off than a Minnesotan.

North Dakota

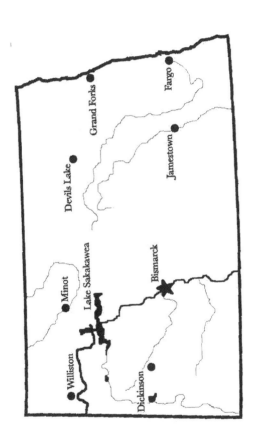

How to Be: **NORTH DAKOTA**
Concealed Carry Permit

The concealed possession of a firearm is a privilege in which many North Dakotans partake. Is it that guy? Or how about that guy over there? Maybe neither. Maybe both! It is this constant state of unknowing about which stranger could at any moment blow your face off that allows North Dakotans to enjoy peace and tranquility.

Much like with a firearm, a permit is required if you plan to conceal this book on your person. Also like a firearm, the knowledge in a book is a weapon. A slow, painless, pointless harmless weapon.

US-15 (10/11)	National Concealed Book License
Attach Picture	Last Name: _____ First Name: _____ Height: ☐ ' ☐☐ " Weight: ☐☐☐ Sex: Y / N D.O.B.: ☐☐ ☐☐ ☐☐☐ Reading Grade Level: ☐

By the No Child Left Behind Act, this permit is suspended within 1,000 feet of a school

Note: The North Dakota Concealed Permit to Carry this book is not reciprocal in CA, CN, HI, IL, MA, MN, MS, NJ, NY, NV, OR, RI, WI.

12

PART A

North Dakota: The Great Back Ground

Being North Dakotan is about more than living upwind of that other Dakota. It's about embodying the values and characteristics of North Dakotans.

Being North Dakotan is not for everyone. It is demanding. It is physical. It is, at times, cruel. Often, it may even seem filled with hypocrisy.

How to Be: NORTH DAKOTA

If statistics are to be believed—as they generally are outside of North Dakota—being North Dakotan will probably not lead you to great fame or fortune.

On the other hand, you and your child will be physically and mentally robust and, thanks to never expecting much out of life, better prepared than almost any other American for the hard times and the inevitable zombie apocalypse.

In short, a North Dakotan is a well rounded person in the sense that he or she is well-mannered, humble, polite, proud, independent, learned and thanks to starchy diets and long winters, actually quite round.

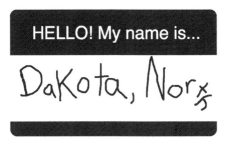

Nice to Make Your Acquaintance

Before getting to the business of becoming North Dakotan, one must understand how the great Peace Garden State came to be America's most envied.

Owing to its majestic, fertile prairie land, North Dakota is often referred to as "The Great Plains." It is also sometimes referred to as the "High Plains," which has more to do with the residency halls at the University of North Dakota in Grand Forks. The state is also occasionally known as the "Plain Plains," a nickname derived from the state's culture. Certain parts of eastern North Dakota are also known as the "Manitoban Baja."

North Dakota claims two major waterways. The Missouri River runs north to south in the western part of the state and the Red River south to north along the eastern border. The Missouri River is so named as it flows to Missouri (or so everyone assumes).

15

The Red River gets its name from the color of the faces of nearby inhabitants during the frequent years it floods its banks, forcing everyone to pump out their basements and buy new furnaces.

A turn of the century illustration of North Dakotans taking part in the annual spring water harvest.

The geography of North Dakota is divided into several major regions. The far east is made up of the Red River Valley. The midwestern portion is the Missouri Plateau. The state's west is called the Badlands, a name given to it because it was impossible to farm. The central portion of the state is made up of formations geographers refer to as "methlabs."

Renowned for its flatness, North Dakota was not always so. During the 1700s it was filled with rolling hills. But early trappers ignorant of conservation loaded them on riverboats and sold them to savvy Eastern traders. The last North Dakota hillpeak was leveled in 1871. North Dakota's hill population never recovered.

North Dakota boasts some of the best Jurassic history anywhere in the United States. One of the most rare, best-preserved fossils ever was found was in an area called "Hell Creek," named for the eventual home of those who believed in dinosaur evolution. Today, the Dakota Dinosaur Museum in Dickinson and the Heritage Center in Bismarck are both excellent places to go and see the giants that roamed the earth alongside Adam and Eve.

What North Dakota lacks in population diversity it makes up for in climate. The difference in degrees between a hot summer day and a cold winter night can be more than 100. These wide swings in temperature keep residents on their toes. On bathroom tile floors, in January, quite literally on their toes.

North Dakota's harsh winter weather is responsible for some of the coldest temperatures ever recorded in the United States. The thermometer often drops dozens of degrees below zero and gets even colder in homes where *you know what you did.*

Low pressure systems sweeping down from Canada are called "Alberta Clippers." These Clippers are far more dangerous than their Los Angeles counterparts. On January 12, 1888, a fast-moving arctic storm known as the "Children's Blizzard," or the "Schoolhouse Blizzard," dropped temperatures 40-some degrees in a matter of hours. Even children toughened by walking to school uphill both ways were killed. The storm resulted in 235 deaths, many of them children walking home from class.

*An 1888 artist's rendering of a teacher cradling a
child, both doomed by the "Children's Blizzard." This
horrible thing actually happened.*

The harsh Arctic winds regularly generate severe windchills
and highway-closing drifts. In the winter these winds blow so
harshly some North Dakotan residents wake up to find themselves in Las Vegas for the weekend.

The state's modern history can be traced back to French-
Canadian adventurer La Vérendrye, who struck out south from
Canada to trade with the region's native tribes, whose larger
selection of big-name retailers, lower sales taxes and better
value after the exchange rate were legendary amongst Canadian
trappers.

18

A Guide to the Plains

The territory that would be North Dakota officially became part of the United States following the Louisiana Purchase of 1803 when Napoleon Bonaparte found himself underwater on the mortgage of a property he had planned to flip before the market went under.

The future state played a large role in Thomas Jefferson's decision to make the purchase, as is evidenced in an 1803 entry in his diary: "Saw exquisite deal today in classified section of 'Le Monde.' Looks like another case of buying more empire than you need. Plenty grassy enough to be reworked for both a back yard for the kids and a classy BBQ station. Appealing. Will look into it tomorrow."

In 1804 Lewis and Clark arrived from the East and traveled through North Dakota, setting up elementary schools named after themselves.

The Sioux are just one of the many Native American tribes that called large areas of what is today North Dakota home. North Dakotans have done much to honor the Sioux tribe, most notably by naming a kick-ass hockey team after them. But also, the state offers such delicious cuisine, the "Siouxper dog," from which one can "Taste the Honor."

Yet, a better understanding of many Sioux customs remains out of grasp of many modern North

Photo of North Dakotan Sioux tribesman in native casual dress.

Dakotans as an outdated reservation system separates the populations, who are forced to arrive and diversify on standby.

"Dakota" is the Sioux word for "always available parking."

A Sioux woman dressed in one of America's first "sexy Pocahontas" Halloween costumes.

A Guide to the Plains

When statehood finally did come in 1889, it did so with controversy.

The 1888 Act by the 50th Congress created the state of North Dakota.

Then a great debate ensued about which Dakota state should be officially admitted first, the North or South? *The New York Post* headline read "North & South: Dakotas Fight Civil War 2."

Too big a star to sign up for the sequel, Abraham Lincoln's part went to up-and-comer Benjamin Harrison, whose performance critics later called "serviceable."

To not play favorites, Harrison asked that the statehood proclamations be shuffled. He then blindly signed them so that it would be unknown which actually become a state first. Today, behavioral scientists argue that it was Harrison's "lottery" treatment of the Dakota proclamations that resulted in both states' reliance on gambling revenues.

Many insist that the state's jagged eastern boundary with Minnesota is due to the Red River of the North. But in fact, the state's founders chose this "torn" look because the wedding planner told them having a right "deckle edge" made a thing fancier.

Early North Dakota politics were defined by widespread corruption and graft. After tiring of writing letters to the editor, a wave of social reformers gained strength and brought with them sweeping legislation that reined in business. Many of these laws were very protectionist in scope and exist to this very day. This creates the paradox of a "red," Republican-leaning state where residents consider themselves paradigms of do-it-yourself, market-driven American conservative values as well as the home of some of the most socialist policies in the nation.

North Dakota's population peaked in 1930 at 680,000. In 1931 the population began a steady decrease which continues to this day. North Dakota's last lynching also happened in 1931. Coincidence?

North Dakota's population is 641,481, not counting undocumented immigrants from Norway.

The state is an important part of America's transportation system. It is home to a great nation-connecting section of the East-West railway known as the Empire Builder. This epic railway runs along the northern edge of North Dakota, putting nearly the whole state, quite literally, on the wrong side of the tracks.

The completion of the Empire Builder allowed the colonization of the West Coast. A flood of immigrants went West looking to put their noses to the grindstone and achieve one of the two American Dreams. One, become instantly wealthy or, two, get a welfare handout in the form a nickel for enough hooch to pass out in the muddy thoroughfare. This flood of travelers riding the Empire Builder came to call North Dakota "trainover country."

A typical mainstream media report from the time plays down the number of jobs created by robber barons.

Within North Dakota the "Empire Builder" railway came to be known as the "Empire Elsewhere Builder."

Today, as other states face economic belt-tightening, North Dakota has found prosperity not in rail development but in energy. With some of the nation's largest oil and coal reserves, North Dakota has profited handsomely from America's reliance on fossil fuels, leading to the state's new nickname: NOPEC.

North Dakota Flag

Adopted in 1911, the flag features a fierce bald eagle grasping seven arrows in one set of talons and an olive branch with three red berries in the other. The arrows represent the state's commitment to defending liberty through armed force while the olive branch represents what the eagle uses to poke you in the eye when it runs out of arrows.

The berries signify that no North Dakotan will ever show up without bars or a hot dish or some food offering. At top are 13 gold stars representing the number of beers the eagle can drink and still "be fine to fly."

In the eagle's beak is a ribbon reading "E PLURIBUS UNUM," which is Latin for "closed on Sunday."

Geografy: It's not Spelling

A true North Dakotan is one who can watch a news report that begins "a man, a deer, and a raccoon were arrested in Grafton last night..." and not immediately ask, "Where is Grafton?"

Geography is important and gives North Dakotans a sense of their place in the world and a better idea of the richness of all the places in the state they will never ever visit.

Additionally, a proper North Dakotan is in touch with the geographic trivia of the state. This command of history allows for engaging cocktail party banter at any social level.

"Did you know Jamestown is home to the world's only albino bison?" That's the kind of conversation starter that makes careers.

A primer on some of North Dakota's geographic highlights.

Rugby

Rugby is violent and a favorite of brutes who enjoy physical confrontation. It is also a sport popular in Europe and Australia.

This is the geographic center of North America, a fact that makes Rugby an interesting addition to any North Dakota road trip. Just outside town, residents erected an obelisk celebrating this distinction. The obelisk has a small marker defining what "obelisk" means.

But there is more to see in Rugby than the obelisk.

For example, have you seen the obelisk? You sure? Why don't you take another look at the obelisk. It's a mighty fine obelisk.

When bringing a teenager to Rugby, be sure to make plenty of lame "you're in the middle of it all now!" jokes. This kind of constant reinforcement that he or she is in the literal middle of nowhere is good for developing the true North Dakotan sense of humility.

Rugby's Pioneer Village and Museum houses a display about Cliff Thompson, known as the "world's tallest Norwegian schoolteacher." Also, because back then teachers weren't the rich, lazy slouches they are today, Thompson was also "the tallest salesman in the world."

Devils Lake

A small city, Devils Lake has the geographic distinction of being the nation's only town with a municipal council that does not recognize apostrophes. The council's reasoning came during the city's name change in 1884 from Creel City to Devils Lake. The 1884 Foundation Committee statement reads, in part, "… that we see apostrophes as an agent of the Italian anarchy movement and will see our community fight such treasonous agitation in all its wicked forms."

While the anarchy movement of the late 19th century withered, Devils Lake's commitment did not. The city, as well as its cultural institutions like Kellys Bar, to this day refuse to recognize the apostrophe's existence.

The Sioux named the nearby lake "mini wak'áŋ chant," meaning "I think my ear just froze and fell off."

Devils Lake is also one of North Dakota's most diverse cities. According to recent census data, it is only 89 percent white.

Jamestown

Jamestown is home to White Cloud and two other rare albino bison. It is also home to the world's largest buffalo statue and the National Buffalo Museum. For some reason, it is known as "The Buffalo City."

Hey boys, for every 100 females age 18 and over in Jamestown, there are only 88 males (and three albino buffalo).

But Jamestown is more than home to Louis L'Amour Writer's Shack and Richard Hieb, who literally got as far as humanly possible from the town by becoming an astronaut. It is also home to White Cloud and two other rare albino bison. It is also home to the world's largest buffalo statue and the National Buffalo Museum.

Did we mention Jamestown is home to White Cloud and the world's largest buffalo statue and the National Buffalo Museum? Okay, just making sure.

A warning: Jamestown residents are sensitive, so take special care to not mistakenly call it "The Bison City."

Minot

Minot became known as "The Magic City" when construction on the great northern railroad came to a stop here during a brutal winter. A tent city erected to shelter workers sprang up quickly, as if "by magic." This tent city also immediately attracted a multitude of whores aiming to service the encamped men, leaving many with "magic" genitals.

The "Saskatchewan Horse" relic from the Canadian sacking of Minot's Dakota Square Mall.

A Guide to the Plains

When the rail workers left in the spring, all the prostitutes remained. Thus, Minot residents today are all descended from prostitutes. Sorru, but that's just an fact.

During Prohibition, Minot was such a central player in the smuggling of booze from Canada, it became known as "Little Chicago." In similar style, Minot resident and master bootlegger Magnus "Paleface" Guvstoffson was brought down on parking ticket charges.

Today Minot is home to many bars as well as an Air Force base and nuclear missile silos--a confluence of drunkenness, provincialism and firepower that makes it maybe the most truly American place on earth.

Also, that famous star from the "Transformers" movies was born here. No, not Shia LaBeouf. No, not Tyrese. No, not Megan Fox. No not Jon Voight. No, not John Tuturro. Yes, that's right, Josh Duhamel!

(Visitors note: Before booking your trip, check to see if Minot is currently celebrating "Noah's Ark Days.")

Grand Forks

Like many of the cities in North Dakota, the area that is now Grand Forks was originally an important Native American trade and social center. The French originally called the city "Les Grandes Fourches" which in English means "a place for bickering about municipal spending."

Legend has it that Grand Forks was established after a steamboat captain named Griggs became stranded by ice and was forced to spend a winter in the area. Like the "Magic City" of Minot, Grand Forks is just one more of North Dakota's most important cities that owes its existence to a few dudes being trapped by absolutely horrendous winter conditions.

Grand Forks takes its sports very seriously and is the home of the world-class Ralph Engelstad Arena also known as "The Ralph." It is also home to the Betty Engelstad Sioux Center. "The Betty." The city is also the home of the lesser-known Willis Ang curling arena, "The Wang." The University of North Dakota Fighting Sioux hockey team is, for all practical purposes, the state's pro franchise.

Recently, the NCAA, citing its policy regarding Native American mascots, demanded that the Sioux retire its name and logo. But the North Dakota legislature countered, passing a law making the retirement of the logo illegal. Leaders were so proud of their defense of the Fighting Sioux name that the governor signed the bill in secret.

Probably a good idea to check with FEMA before planning a visit.

Theodore Roosevelt National Park (a.k.a The Badlands)

Established in 1978, this national park is named for President Theodore "Not the Wheelchair One" Roosevelt. It carries his namesake because the president had worked in this section of the Badlands as a young man. His experience in this unforgiving ecosystem where almost nothing of value can live, let alone flourish, perfectly prepared him for national politics.

Dickinson

According to many Americans, none of the extraordinary dinosaur fossils found near Dickinson exist. So there is no reason to go here.

The International Peace Garden
Established in 1932, the garden straddles the border of the United States and Canada and represents an international show of good faith. The stone slab anchoring the garden reads "we two nations / dedicate this garden / and pledge ourselves / that as long as men / shall live, we will / not take up arms / against one another." Twenty years later, the United States placed hundreds of nuclear-armed intercontinental ballistic missiles within a few miles of the garden.

Williston
Best known for its municipal motto "What you Talkin' 'Bout Williston?," the city is near Lake Sakakawea and home to both Fort Union Trading Post and Fort Buford historical sites. The area's other attraction, "The Confluence," is so named as the spot where the Yellowstone and Missouri rivers come together and conflue. Also, oil. Lots and lots of oil.

Williston is home to a true geographic oddity. About a half mile north of the city proper is a hill that can be walked up, both ways. There is a schoolhouse at one side of the hill. For grade-school-age children, walk them up this hill, both ways, and constantly berate them: "Believe me now?!"

Wahpeton
Wahpeton is an important migratory area for a number of species, including waterfowl passing to and from Canada and Minnesotans escaping Minnesota tax policy. Wahpeton is a great place to hunt either.

University of North Dakota Fighting Sioux, Baltimore Colt and "Greatest Game Ever Played" kicker Steve Myhra was born in Wahpeton.

Bismarck

The state capital, Bismarck is the second largest city in North Dakota. Bismarck is the factory that makes the laws and regulations of the state. It cannot be outsourced.

Like every other city in America over 100 years old, Bismarck burned to the ground at one time. Maybe like the 1920s. It seems like a lot of things burned down then.

Originally called Edwinton, Bismarck changed its name in 1873 to honor the great Otto Von Bismarck. The city's namesake German chancellor once said "There is a Providence that protects idiots, drunkards, children, and the United States of America."

A Guide to the Plains

Black Hills

A short jaunt across he border into South Dakota, the Black Hills consist of a geological rock core of Paleozoic, Mesozoic, Cenozoic and Booooringzoic material. The Hills became important in the 1970s when locals, fevered from having watched hours of Fox News commercials, prospected here and found great gold deposits.

Don't be fooled by the name; it is an entirely safe neighborhood to visit.

Mandan

The beer to Bismarck's bump, "Mandan" is derived from the Native American tribe of the same name that once called the banks of this section of the Missouri River home. In this respect, Bismarck and Mandan are like the cities of Buda and Pest, coming together across the Danube to create one of the most architecturally and culturally wealthy cities in the world. Except without any of the second part of that sentence.

In 1974, Mandan won a lawsuit with the National Organization for Women who had tried to rename the city Persondan.

Fort Mandan

The location where, in 1804, the Lewis and Clark expedition wimped out in the face of temperatures touching 45 degrees below zero. The fort's exact location is not known. Its replica stands near Washburn, ND.

The fort represents an extraordinary point in the Lewis and Clark expedition where the native Mandan tribe helped the explorers through the incredibly harsh winter. The tribe was repaid years later with a smallpox epidemic carried by an American Fur Company steamboat. You're welcome, Mandans.

Valley City

Valley City is called the "City of Bridges" for the numerous structures spanning the Sheyenne River. There is the West City Park Bridge, City Park Bridge, Rainbow Bridge, Hospital Bridge, Highline Bridge, Mill Dam Bridge, Maryvale Bridge and the VCSU Footbridge. The city's Beau Bridges seemed promising early on but was later eclipsed by another Bridges.

Lake Sakakawea

The third largest man-made lake in the U.S., Sakakawea was created with the establishment of the Garrison Dam in the 1950s. Lake Sakakawea is named after the Shoshone woman of the same name who assisted Lewis and Clark from Fort Mandan during that tubular backpacking trip they took after college. (She is also known as Sacagawea.) Sacagawea left her people and assisted the explorers as they traveled westward. Charbonneau, Sacagawea's European husband who married her at age 13, could not go along as he was a registered sex offender.

In addition to being remembered with the name of a lake, Sacagawea has been honored with a federal coin, which can be traded for a can of Coca-Cola.

Medora

Medora is one of the most popular tourist attractions in the state. It was named in 1883 by French nobleman Marquis de Mores for his wife Medora von Hoffman, making Medora the Taj Mahal of North Dakota. The city is also home to the famed Medora Musical cowboy stage musical, making Medora the gayest city in the state.

Medora is the entryway to Theodore Roosevelt National Park, the Cowboy Hall of Fame, Maah Daah Hey Trail, the Pitchfork

A Guide to the Plains

Fondue festival, the Bully Pulpit Golf Course, and the Harold Schafer Heritage Center. Do not try to do them all in one day.

When traveling through many of Medora's tourist-engineered sites, ask your children if they understand the irony in the fact that Medora started as a meat processing facility.

Grafton
Grafton has offered $20,000 grants to anyone who buys or builds a new single family home, townhouse or condo. Meanwhile, visitors get nothing.

New Town
The picturesque heart of Lake Sakakawea. Not known for its creativity.

Parshall
Called the "Saudi Arabia of North America," Parshall is a town of just 1,000 that discovered significant oil reserves and has since become a boom town. It is also one North Dakota place where the residents mean something completely different when they call their town "boring."

Fargo
Established as a set for the 1996 Oscar-winning film, Fargo is now the largest city in the state. Known for their intense attention to detail, the filmmakers gave the city an elaborate backstory.

Thanks to its lenient marriage laws, Fargo was known as the Divorce Capital of the Midwest in the 1880s. While it seems this was a smear against the city, it actually signified great progressiveness, the general method of "divorce" in the region at the time being throwing the unwanted wife in a well.

Today, Fargo remains North Dakota's engine of social progress, a single-cylinder, 22-horse-power, engine of progress.

As Fargo boomed, thanks to the railroad, it began to compete in importance with other Midwest cities. Things soon got out of hand. Jealous of Chicago's 1871 version, Fargo's mayor declared that "Those Shytown bastards haven't seen a thing" and threw his lit cigar in an oil barrel. The subsequent "Kinda' Great Fargo Fire" of 1893 was a letdown, resulting in only a portion of the damage residents had hoped for. Fifty years later, a tornado would do a much better job; but by that time Chicago's lead was cemented.

If you're looking to get mugged, eat sushi, or engage in any one of a number of activities available in most any major city, Fargo is the place in North Dakota to do it.

Finally, it is noteworthy that the terminology "Fargo-Class" refers to both a type of Naval cruiser characterized by a pyramidal superstructure with single-trunked funnel intended to improve AA gun arcs of fire as well as a type of Fargo resident's body shape typified by its similarity to said Naval vessel.

West Fargo

Known as Fargo's New Jersey, visitors to the city are advised not to engage the locals in a conversation about property taxes.

North Dakota Government

As the one covering North Dakota government, this chapter is inevitably larger than it should be. Also, in line with the political leanings of the state's residents, this chapter will endeavor to do a limited amount for you. The rest of the learning about North Dakota's government should be done by yourself, as our founding fathers intended.

North Dakota is represented by two senators in Washington D.C. It has one delegate to the U.S. House of Representatives. One very, very lonely delegate whom the other members of congress avoid because he smells like beets.

North Dakota's state system of government is modeled after that of the United States, with the Governor serving as head of state. As with the federal model, this makes him to blame for everything.

Governor Lynn Frazier was the first state leader ever to be recalled in the history of American government. Immediately after his recall, Frazier was elected to the U.S. Senate.

Also like the national system, North Dakota's government features a legislature that is bicameral. This lifestyle choice means the legislature has few discrimination protections under state law.

The state House of Representatives and state Senate also maintain the national model, with the latter looking down on the former, literally; state senators must be at least six feet tall to serve.

North Dakota Political Positions and Roles

Governor
Roles: Practice signature with multiple pens and must always wear a tie. Fly over floods in helicopter. Groom mustache for reelection. The most North Dakotan of all North Governors was Ole Olson.

Lieutenant Governor
Roles: The dating coach of the legislature, maintains legislative relations. During election years, "brings the crazy" with which the candidates for governor simply cannot in good conscience associate themselves.

Secretary of State
Roles: Custodian of the state's Great Seal. Responds to governor's requests to "take a memo." Ben Meier was the longest ever serving secretary of state in the nation, holding the office for 34 years.

State Auditor
Roles: Audits state, duh.

Attorney General
Roles: Represents the state government in all lawyer jokes. How does one become North Dakota's attorney general? Go to law school and be named George or William; 18 percent of all the state's AGs held those names.

Insurance Commissioner
Roles: Position the state's insurance policies in a manner that will best insure a job for the Insurance Commissioner after stepping down.

Tax Commissioner
Roles: He That Will Not Be Named is the archenemy of the taxpayer. For their transgressions against taxpaying North Dakotans, former ND tax commissioners Byron Dorgan and Kent Conrad were both banished to Washington DC to suffer the Senatorial purgatory of never accomplishing anything of meaning.

Superintendent of Public Instruction
Roles: Whatever happens, never ever never hand out condoms in school.

State Cabinet
Roles: Keep governor's liquor out of sight. Balance lamp.

President pro Tempore
Roles: Preside over the Senate when the Lieutenant Governor goes to take a leak. "Pro tempore" is a fancy way to say "for the time being," but it makes the officer holder feel better.

Speaker of the House
Roles: Never, ever, never shuts up.

Putting the Pit in Capital: Bismarck

The state capital since 1883, Bismarck, much like North Dakota for homesteaders, was not the first choice.

After statehood, to move the capital closer to the state's population, lawmakers chose Jamestown as the new center of government. But late one night, Bismarck partisans stole the state records back to Bismarck and held them captive until the legislature convened there again. God punished this by burning Bismarck to the ground in 1898. Jamestown then let Bismarck keep the capital, saying "it needs it more than we do."

The Michelin Guide to Capitals gave Bismarck a review of "bland, but adequate."

Photographic proof from the Library of Congress that despite common accusations the state capital is not a "one horse town."

North Dakota is called a "red" state, owing to its electorate's preference for Republicans and the color that electorate's face turns after those Republicans take office and begin governing.

Republicans currently hold supermajorities in the House, Senate, and the fourth floor bathroom. The leading party does make an effort to reach across the aisle, usually to take some dumb Democrat's lunch.

A political cartoon from 1916 proves the subtle rhetoric of political discourse has not changed all that much in 100 years.

NDGOP is both the state's Republican Party and a crummy Scrabble hand. The party was once the Independent Voters Association, a group of independent North Dakotans who all independently voted for the exact same people every time.

The Democratic party is also known as the NPL, or Non-Partisan League. It is just like the Justice League in that it has the name "League" in its name.

NoDaktivity: Let's Play Tea Party

Unlike tea parties played by most of the rest of the nation's youth, to "play tea party" means something distinctively different in North Dakota. While it is true that some children of pointy-headed liberal elites at the University of North Dakota play "tea party" with cups and saucers, most of the state's children play tea party the true North Dakotan way.

You will need: Cardboard for signs. Paper. Glue. Markers, Sprinkles. A valid concealed carry permit for a handgun.

How to play:

Tell your child about some apparent injustice to liberty. A good start is "It is my constitutional right to have my dessert first." Next, have your child call a few of his or her friends to get together on the lawn. For this activity, the children should all make signs with catchy phrases wittily summing up their positions. Below are some starter ideas:

- I Voted for Ice Cream not Cream of Broccoli.
- Hands off my Everything.
- Meals not Meatloaf!
- Diaper Change we can believe in!
- Corn is Scorn!
- The only thing trickling down is on my leg.
- You know who else liked Bedtime? Hitler.

The first child to successfully compare a parent's behavior to Hitler's wins!

It's Jake Preus
or Socialism

To turn back the red wave from North Dakota the Republicans of Minnesota chose the following men. They are your only hope. At the primaries, June 21,

CONCENTRATE ON THE REPUBLICAN CONVENTION CANDIDATES

FOR GOVERNOR **J. A. O. PREUS**		**X**
FOR LIEUTENANT GOVERNOR **LOUIS L. COLLINS**		**X**
FOR SECRETARY OF STATE **MIKE HOLM**		**X**
FOR STATE TREASURER **HENRY RINES**		**X**
FOR ATTORNEY GENERAL **CLIFFORD L. HILTON**		**X**
FOR RAILROAD AND WAREHOUSE COMMISSIONER **O. P. B. JACOBSON**		**X**

SMASH SOCIALISM!

Tourists: The Modern Dakota Trapping

Like the worst "ism"-- antidisestablishmentarianism --North Dakota in-state tourism takes longer to complete than should be necessary and doesn't make a lot of sense afterward. The distance between where you live and the city you've been told is "not all that bad" is often hundreds of miles. A little research before making a trip can make all the difference.

City: **Dickinson**
Motto: "The Western Edge"
Percentage Truth to Motto: 90% (inside ND) / 27% (Outside ND)
Upside: Badlands
Downside: Is at "the Western edge"
Miles from Fargo: 292
Olive Garden?: No

How to Be: NORTH DAKOTA

City: **Beulah**
Motto: "It's all right here"
Percentage Truth to Motto: 8%
Upside: Coal mine tours; "abundant" RV parking
Downside: All of it literally right here in front of you
Miles from Fargo: 275
Olive Garden?: No

City: **Jamestown**
Motto: "More to Explore"
Percentage Truth to Motto: 15%
Upside: "1,000 memories."
Downside: One memory short of worthwhile amount
Miles from Fargo: 97
Olive Garden?: No

City: **Minot**
Motto: "Discover the Magic"
Percentage Truth to Motto: 34%
Upside: Water sports; "Affordable"
Downside: Likely first city burned to ground during Canadian invasion
Miles from Fargo: Like, a bazillion
Olive Garden?: No

City: **Fargo**
Motto: "Always Warm"
Percentage Truth to Motto: 0.0%
Upside: Numerous strip clubs
Downside: Numerous strip clubs
Miles from Fargo: 0
Olive Garden?: Yes!

A Guide to the Plains

City: **Ellendale**
Motto: "Gateway of North Dakota"
Percentage Truth to Motto: 48%
Upside: Birding.
Downside: Not a good place to be a bird
Miles from Fargo: 159
Olive Garden?: No

City: **Towner**
Motto: "Cattle Capital of North Dakota"
Percentage Truth to Motto: 99%
Upside: Denbigh Experimental Forest
Downside: Not actually in Towner County
Miles from Fargo: Might as well be 350,000
Olive Garden?: No

City: **Williston**
Motto: "Experience the Outdoors. Live the Adventure."
Real Motto: Oil!
Percentage Truth to Motto: 110,000 barrels per day
Upside: Oil!; $2,000 signing bonuses at McDonald's
Downside: Oil!
Miles from Fargo: I said, oil
Olive Oil?: Also, yes

NoDaktivity: Become Governor

Nothing is more fun than being governor of a state That is especially true when you're the top politician in a state as politically important as North Dakota.

To play, first cut along the dotted line of the mustache.

THIS SIDE DOWN

Using tape or glue or the gum in your mouth, attach the mustache onto your upper lip.

Now walk around the house and orate:

"Working together, in the last legislative session, we set aside $200 million in our Budget Stabilization Fund, and another $200 million in our Permanent Oil Tax Trust Fund. As I speak to you today, we have set forth a plan to begin the next biennium with reserves of $600 million and to grow those reserves to between $800 million and $1.2 billion."

Fun!

The Worldly North Dakotan

Just because you live in North Dakotan doesn't mean you cannot deeply understand and appreciate global culture. Indeed, North Dakota is home to numerous cities and locations that, while not the places themselves, have the exact same names.

A list of locations in North Dakota that will allow you to declare "I've been to Munich!" and not be a liar:

Place: Munich, ND
Equivalent: Munich, Germany

Place: Lisbon, ND
Equivalent: Lisbon, Portugal

Place: Hague, ND
Equivalent: Hague (The), Netherlands

Place: Wimbledon, ND

How to Be: NORTH DAKOTA

Equivalent: Wimbledon, England

Place: Berlin, ND
Equivalent: Berlin, Germany

Place: Calia, ND
Equivalent: Calia, Paraguay

Place: Edinburg, ND
Equivalent: Edinburgh, Scotland

Place: Hamburg, ND
Equivalent: Hamburg, Germany

Place: Leeds, ND
Equivalent: Leeds, England

Place: Perth, ND
Equivalent: Perth, Australia

Place: Pisek, ND
Equivalent: Pisek, Czech Republic

Place: St. Thomas, ND
Equivalent: St. Thomas, Virgin Islands

Place: Verona, ND
Equivalent: Verona, Italy

Place: Zeeland, ND
Equivalent: Zeeland, Netherlands

Place: Riverdale, ND
Equivalent: Rivendell, Middle Earth

Zoology: A North Dakota Setchbook

You can't spell Zoology without "gee," as in "Gee, what the heck is that thing? Can I shoot it?"

But North Dakota's animal kingdom is more than the things a person is allowed to shoot and the things a person has to shoot in secret. The state is home to animals as diverse as the colors found in a peacock's plume. (Note: North Dakota has no peacocks.)

For example, species include the flickertail, a small prairie rodent known for the way its tail often "flicks" due to diabetes from its native diet of Widman's chocolate covered potato chips.

From brown birds to slightly different brown colored birds, a trek through the North Dakota wilderness can reveal a splendid medley of wildlife. A cross section of some of the state's more characteristic and unique creatures.

Buffalo / Bison

These bovine ungulates were hunted to near extinction with the last wild herds gone from North Dakota's plains by 1880. President Ulysses S. Grant vetoed a conservation bill in 1874 after pressure from the populist "Kill Baby Kill" movement and in part because Native Americans depended on bison for food. And he was the "good" general.

Buffalo Grass
A groovy drought-tolerant forage shortgrass native to North Dakota. Authorities do not consider "I didn't know it was there" a valid excuse for growing this in your home.

Prairie Warbler
Commonly found on the plains, prairie warblers live in open cup nests and have two categories of songs: One low pitch; the other buzzy and ascending.

Prairie Wobbler
Commonly found on the plains, prairie wobblers live in the bottle. Their song is always the same.

Caterpillar (brown and black)
This creature is vital to the ecology of the state. Be careful not
to squish it!

Caterpillar (yellow):
This creature is vital to the economy of the state. Be careful not to let it squish you!

Red Fox
Largest of the true foxes. The red fox is a icon of late night
North Dakotan TV reruns.

58

Great Horned Owl
A master of its own freedom, the great horned owl's throaty squeak has been called the only truly American bird call.

Canadian Goose
South-migrating animal that is increasingly considered a pest as they congregate in public spaces like golf courses and parking lots. Can be aggressive.

Windsor Canadians
South-migrating animal that is increasingly considered a pest as they congregate in public spaces like golf courses and parking lots. Can be aggressive.

Elk
Sociable animals that prefer to live and feed in tight-knit herds. Except during mating season, the males prefer to group together away from females. Known for unique social rituals.

Benevolent and Protective Order of Elks
Sociable animals that prefer to live and feed in tight-knit herds. Except during mating season, the males prefer to group together away from females. Known for unique social rituals.

63

Bald Eagle
Haliaeetus leucocephalus!!!

NoDaktivity: Spot the Difference on Highway 2

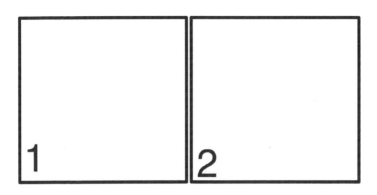

Can you spot the four differences between these two pictures of traffic on Highway 2 during a blizzard?

ANSWERS

1) The truck carrying a load of potatoes in Picture 1 is carrying beets in Picture 2.

2) The Pontiac driver in Picture 1 has a blood alcohol level of .04. In Picture 2 it is .19.

3) It is night in Picture 2.

4) In Picture 2 there is a deer directly in front of your car. It is not there in Picture 1.

NoDaktivity: North Dakota Maze

Dale is sick and tired of shoveling snow in Grand Forks. His brother-in-law has a Phoenix timeshare. Can you help get him through the maze to get out of North Dakota?

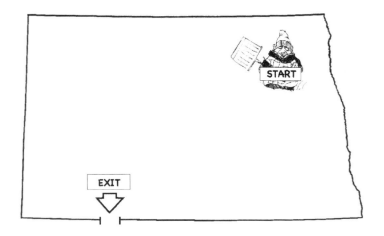

Famous North Dakotans

William "Bill" Owens
If you are not inspired by a man born and raised in maybe the most landlocked state in the nation who went on to become an admiral in the United States Navy, it's hopeless.

Warren Christopher
Born in Scranton, Warren Minor Christopher served important offices under presidents Lyndon Johnson, Jimmy Carter, and Bill Clinton before dying in Los Angeles in 2011. The exact reasons for his death are unknown, though most North Dakotans suspect "shame."

Phil Jackson

Phil Jackson is a hall of fame NBA player and coach who won numerous championships with the Lakers and Bulls. Jackson was aided in his success by his North Dakotan upbringing, which instantly made him comfortable ordering a bunch of African Americans around.

Theodore Roosevelt

Theodore "Teddy" Roosevelt is one of North Dakotas most famous residents, despite really not having spent that much time there. In face, it is unlikely the amount of time Roosevelt spent on his ranch north of Medora would even qualify him for in-state tuition.

While many celebrate Roosevelt's time in the state, most forget exactly what circumstances made him choose North Dakota. The Rough Rider decided to ranch in the bleak western plain following the near simultaneous deaths of his mother and wife in New York City. The Badlands looked mighty good then, apparently.

The terrible winter of 1886-1887 wiped out his entire herd and Roosevelt hightailed it back to the East Coast, but not before taking lots of pictures of himself with guns looking rough and tough. After just one season or so in North Dakota, Teddy ran for New York City mayor as "The Cowboy of the Dakotas." Roosevelt said, "The worst of all fears is the fear of living... in the Badlands."

As is well documented, Roosevelt loved to talk. While in North Dakota, Roosevelt earned the Native American name "Mustache Always-Moving."

The bottom line is that by the time you complete this book, you will be as North Dakotan as Teddy Roosevelt.

Moden Valley City newcomers named after the Savior prefer "Jesus" over "Christ."

Christ Paetou

In 1878, this Valley City resident weighed in at 448 pounds, making him the heaviest man in the Dakota Territoty. A slacker by modern standards, Paetou wouldn't even be the heaviest man in Valley City.

Lawrence Welk
Like Miller is the "'Champagne of beer," The Lawrence Welk Show was "Champagne Music."

Welk was born in Strasburg, ND, the son of immigrant home-steaders. Young Lawrence weathered his first North Dakota under an overturned wagon insulated by sod, an experience that prepared him for show business. The polka's Luke Sky-walker, Welk promised his dad he would work the family farm until he was 21 in exchange for a $400 accordion.

Louis L'Amour
Born Louis Dearborn LaMoore in Jamestown, ND "where the long grass blows." Credited with 89 novels, L'Amour was as much a text farmer as a writer. He maintained his connection to the hard scrabble life of his frontier stories by living in Los Angeles. L'Amour's stories were so popular, many were made into films, including "Hondo," starring John Wayne as a princi-pled army soldier, and "Lando," about the rakish governor of a mining colony who has to choose between prosperity and friendship.

Dick Armey
A house majority leading congressman and an architect of the "Republican Revolution," Dick was born in Cando, ND. In 1994, he worked with Newt Gingrich to draft the "Contract with America," which the nation later had to pay a penalty to get out of when it wanted to switch government providers. Armey went on to found FreedomWorks, which had nothing, absolutely nothing, to do with launching the grass roots tea party movement.

He is the half brother of Vagina Navy.

While its popularity inside the state won Oddmund T. Engebretsen great local fame, his "Mr. Potato-Vodka Head" never took off outside North Dakota.

Chuck Klosterman

Author of the book "Fargo Rock City," Klosterman is the Woody Allen of North Dakota, in that people from outside the state associate him with North Dakota far more than do the people inside the state.

Roger Maris

A grown man who was paid handsomely to hit a ball with a stick.

Woodrow Wilson Keeble

Born and raised in Waubay and Wahpeton, Keeble was one of the Army's most decorated veterans. He ignored numerous wounds during Korean War fighting to win a Purple Heart, a Silver Star and the Medal of Honor. On October 20, 1951, "Dakota Rambo" single-handedly took out three machine-gun bunkers and another seven enemy troops all with only half his nose left after a grenade blast. His regiment called him "The 14 Points… of Entry to your Abdomen."

Suffering from Tuberculosis, Keeble returned to the States where one of the nation's greatest warriors was finally defeated by the American healthcare system.

Kellan Lutz

Not all of the beef that leaves the state is from a slaughter-house.

Northo Dakotans are not born, they're made, after being born.

Turning an adorable 8-pound blob of fat and no hair into a grizzled 308-pound blob of fat with no hair takes hard work, commitment, love, and cream of mushroom soup. Lots of cream of mushroom soup.

NoDaktivity: What's Your North Dakota Name?

Many who have moved away from North Dakota or do not have Scandinavian heritage have never known the joys of life with a solid North Dakotan surname. This is easily remedied.

To your last name attach any one of the below suffixes. For an extra prairie pizzazz, add umlauts to any letter "a" "u" and a slash through any letter "o."

Suffixes

-sson	-rud	-svärd
-björn	-holm	-gaard
-qvis	-strom	-staad

For example: "Martinez" becomes "Märtinezstrom," or "Märtinezgaard." While "Muhammad" becomes "Mühämmädsson," "Mühämmädrud," or "Mühämmädholm."

Congratulations Jeremiah Røsenbäümbjorn and Mei Li Wøngqvist, you're North Dakotans!

Pregnancy: A North Dakota Condition

Congratulations on your pregnancy / immaculate conception!

While the most important steps to raising a proper North Dakotan occur after birth, there are a few key things you can do now to ensure a healthy child, besides, of course, staying fully carbohydrated.

Beet Baths

While many know of the Dead Sea mud bath, few outside the state have heard of the healing qualities of the beet bath. Place three pails-full of fresh beets into very hot water and let stew for ten minutes. Enter the bath and soak. Stretch marks. Sore back. Indigestion. Hemorrhoids. All might be cured by this legendary beet bath. Why not?

Smartening

Evidence now exists of a connection between the sounds a baby hears in utero and the type of child he or she turns out to be. For example, science has shown a baby that is exposed to Mozart during gestation more often than not turns out to be a pretentious prick. A North Dakota child should be exposed to the sounds of the state, including prairie winds on tall wheat, the song of the Western Meadowlark and geese, the hoot of a passing train, and old men complaining about every last thing imaginable.

This book's accompanying CD of sounds for the pregnant North Dakotan, will be released sometime in the future.

Cold Weather Preparation

Starting in the third trimester, packing ice around your swollen belly will prepare your child for the rigors of North Dakotan winters. A mom-to-be should lie on her side and carefully place bags of ice around the stomach. These bags should remain in place until 20 minutes after feeling is lost in the skin. If the mother happens to be lucky enough to be pregnant during winter, an acceptable alternative is to go outside and lie face down in a snow drift.

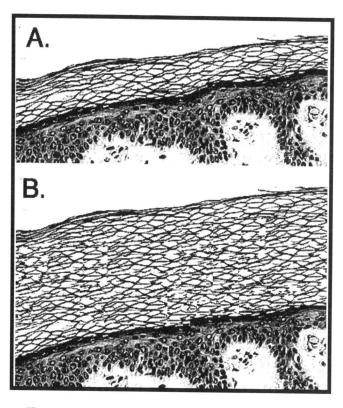

Figure A. Microscopic view of average human dermis.

Figure B. Microscopic view of North Dakotan dermis.

Hospital "Go" Bag

When the time comes for the four hour drive to the nearest hospital, you will want to have a "go bag." In addition to a change of clothing, there are a few other items to consider packing. A checklist:

- Winch
- VFW Hall Coupons
- Agreed-upon name list
- Secret name list
- Wife
- Heath Insurance Card
- Portable radio
- List of radio channels playing the Sioux game
- Six Pack (Note: Most hospitals are neither on- nor off-sale.)

Naming a North Dakota Baby

North Dakotans are liberal when it comes to baby names, accepting both spellings of Stacy / Stacie and Jodi / Jody.

According to the Census Bureau, by the 1960s "Jody" rose to be one of the top 100 most popular boy names in the upper Midwest. Though its popularity has declined, naming your boy Jody is still one of the biggest head starts you can give him on his way to playing professional hockey.

To answer the question, yes, naming your North Dakota child "Dakota" is overkill.

Health Insurance

Didn't establish residency in Minnesota in time to get its state-sponsored health insurance? No worries. Cut out the prepared card below and present it when you arrive at the hospital. By the time they figure it out, you'll be back on the highway on the way home.

BlueCross BlueShield
of North Dakota

4510 13th Avenue S.
Fargo, North Dakota 58121-0001

Member Name: Rufus Skywalker Roosevelt III
ID: 230843-9-2

Medical and Rx Benefits   Emergency:$50
RxBIN: 6492o03   Office Visit:$35

Additional Co-Pays May Apply   ™

NoDaktivity: Potty Training: You "Can" Doo It

A North Dakota boy is considered completely potty trained when a full 87 percent of his bodily waste makes it into the toilet.

A North Dakota girl is considered completely potty trained when she can go to the bathroom without producing any sound whatsoever.

North Dakotan children love the great out(house) doors.

Homesteading

Signed into law by Abraham Lincoln, The Homestead Act granted 160 acres of land outside the original 13 colonies to anyone who applied for and worked it. America's original "Free iPod!" scam, the program settled nearly 300,000,000 acres between the 1860s and 1980s.

Homesteading played a pivital role in settling North Dakota. From 1879 until statehood, more than 100,000 homesteaders came to the state and another 250,000 arrived between1895 and 1914.

Of course, homesteading in North Dakota wasn't all wine and roses. In fact homesteaders drank stagnant puddle water instead of wine and gave their beloveds nettles instead of roses. This may account for how young North Dakota women are often said to be "itching to get married."

Homesteading got its name from the combination of "home" and "instead of," because what homesteaders got when they arrived at their North Dakota parcel was something "instead of" a home. Homesteading was also hard work. Most arrived to their parcels with no shelter and little food. Without the Today Show's Al Roker to jovially prepare them, they had a stupefying ignorance of what the winters would bring.

Many North Dakotan children have great-grandparents who can still bore them to tears with tales of nearly freezing to death and working 40-hour days in 60-below temperatures farming dirt for the dirt market. Sadly, most North Dakotan children no longer experience frostbite and early onset rheumatism.

Hosting a Homesteader Night is a fun and easy way to help your little North Dakotans-in-training grasp what it was like when their "X-box" was the pine container a child was buried in when he or she died of smallpox.

First, if possible, pick a night in the winter. To prepare for the night, turn off the heat and open all the windows. Ideally, you want to be wearing at least three layers at the warmest point in the day.

Prepare your family's normal breakfast, lunch and dinner. But then throw half of it away before eating. Homesteading families rarely had enough to eat and commonly went through their days and nights with pangs of hunger. Children of the time called these "tummy ouchies."

If your children complain for a snack, give them some candle wax and tell them it is homesteader "Bubble Yum." If you have some hard candies ready, you can distribute two to each child. Be sure to say "Merry Christmas" when you do this.

It would require about 13,500 "Homestead Act" commemroative stamps to express mail yourself back to New York City.

During the day, all children over the age of five should be put to work. If you don't have any necessary work around the house, have each one dig and refill a hole in the yard 40 or 50 times. Children younger than five can spend the day playing in the dirt pile.

At bedtime, after blowing out the candles (electricity is off-limits), the entire family should retire to a small square on the floor where you will all sleep huddled under as many blankets as you can find. Sharing warmth to survive the night? Now that's family bonding! For even more reality, have everyone forgo showering or bathing for several days before bunking down together.

If you have a family with two or more children, wake one up in the middle of the night and have him or her go to bed upstairs. Tell the rest of the family that he or she is dead of typhoid. A little later, mom should dismiss herself for the night. Dad should explain that mom died in childbirth and will not be participating anymore, ever.

To develop true sympathy for what earlier North Dakotan children endured, homesteading night should go on for numerous days.

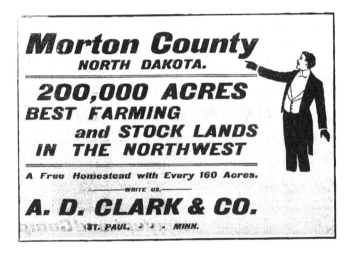

Manners: The Foundation of North Dakota's Incredibly Awesome Humility

A proper North Dakotan can always be identified by his or her exquisite manners. These manners are based on three core principles.

1)_I'm Fine
A proper North Dakotan will always turn down the offer of anything from anyone who is not his or her parent. Want some help cutting that grass? "No thanks. I'm fine." Want a vine to grab onto to get out of that quicksand? "No thanks. I'm fine."

The minimum number of times a proper North Dakotan child should turn down any offer before accepting is five. If the offer is only extended four times, it wasn't needed that badly, was it?

2) It Could be Worse
You betcha' it could.

The core of a North Dakotan understanding about the world is that it could be worse.

Think it's cold today? Could be worse. Think there's nothing to do in this small town? Could be worse. That smell drifting over from the beet sugar refinery? Could be worse.

3) How's your weather?

At the heart of how a state of opinionated, easily offended residents go about their days without constantly getting into arguments is the ability to talk about the weather.

The weather plays no favorites. Unlike taxes or reproductive rights, your neighbor's opinion of it doesn't matter to you. Talking about the weather also gives grandparents and grand-children something to do for more than six minutes. It is the vanilla ice cream of conversation.

A flowchart demonstrates the lifecycle of of a North Dakotan conversation.

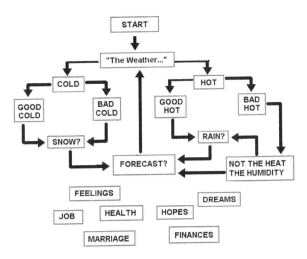

NoDaktivity: Make Your Own Beet Sugar

During the Napoleonic Wars, much of Europe was cut off from its sweet, sweet Caribbean sugar supply. Enter the humble beet, which can be refined into delicious sugar without any of the pesky ancillary troubles of the sugarcane trade, such as warm weather and white sand beaches.

Today 30 percent of the world's sugar comes from beets. North Dakota is one of the largest sugar beet producers nationwide, accounting for nearly 6 million tons per year, or about 9.3 tons per every North Dakotan.

Beet farming and sugaring is a fundamental of the North Dakota economy. The industry is sweetened by the federal quotas and subsidies that guarantee a market for beet sugar. As famed market championing economist Adam Smith wrote in "The Wealth of Nations": "It is the maxim of every prudent master of a family, never to attempt to make at home what it will cost him more to make than to buy, unless such making is underwritten by ag subsidies which guarantee reelection to the legislative body."

As a bonus, sugar beet processing facilities emit a delicious aroma treasured by generations of North Dakotans. Ask any resident who has lived near a Crystal Sugar plant, and he or she will tell you.

But factory farmers shouldn't get all the government sugar pork. Below is a simple recipe for making beet sugar in your own kitchen.

What You'll Need
- Two pounds of sugar beets
- Pan
- Colander or strainer
- Mom's permission

1) Wash and/ or scrub beets.
2) Chop beets into small pieces.
3) Place beets in a large pot. Add enough water to prevent them sticking.
4) Cook until beets soften and lose color.
5) Strain beets, saving the juice. (Boiled beets can be saved for delicious Borscht!)
6) Put juice back on the burner and simmer it until thick and syrupy. Stir constantly.
7) Let cool. Syrup will start to crystallize. Cover with a towel or cloth. Let sit overnight.
8) Remove crystallized beet sugar from pan, breaking it up into smaller granules.
9) Submit your request for subsidy to the U.S. Department of Agriculture, 1400 Independence Ave., S.W., Washington, DC 20250

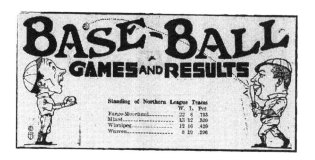

The Sporting North Dakotan

North Dakotan athletes always put on their game faces to bring an "A" game 110 percent of the time because they just want it more, even though they're also always sure to just take it one game at a time. And when the game gets tough, North Dakotan athletes reach down in the basement, which they often have to pump first.

Because it lacks high profile sports teams, many believe the state isn't interested in athletics. While it's true a North Dakota newspaper's use of "barn burner" is just as often literal as not, the state is quite sporting.

89

The state's tailgating traditons have not changed all that much in the last century.

Pro Sports

There is no "I" in team, but there is also no "team" in "North Dakota."

With a state too small to support a major sports franchise, North Dakotans face the humiliating prospect of cheering for Minnesota's Twins, Vikings, Wild and whatever Minneapolis' NBA team is called.

The advantage of being a Minnesota sports fan is that, if the team loses, a North Dakotan can cheer because Minnesota lost. But if the team wins, North Dakotans cheer out of regionalism. Better Minnesota than New York. The upside of Minnesota winning is of course an academic hypothetical.

An increasing number of North Dakota residents cheer for the Dallas Cowboys. You can usually find this tight knit group of fans standing in a Home Depot parking lot early in the morning waiting to be picked up for work.

Hockey

North Dakota's real pro sports franchise is the University of North Dakota Fighting Sioux hockey team.

The less controversial Lover-Not-a-Fighter Sioux mascot.

One of the state's most popular sports, hockey combines the speed of basketball, the thrilling goal-line drama of soccer, the physicality of football, and the mullets of NASCAR.

Hockey traces its beginnings to a number of early European games such as shinty, shinney, hurley and alcoholism. Windsor, Nova Scotia, Montreal, Quebec, Kingston, and Ontario all claim to be the site of the first game of "hockey." While the sport may have been invented in Canada, it was perfected in the United States when it was used to defeat communism.

No self-respecting adult can consider his or her child North Dakotan unless that child plays hockey. The rise of the "hockey mom" as a national demographic came as a shock to many North Dakota women who had always understood "hockey mom" to mean "a mom."

A Sioux warrior holds a traditional prayer for victory over the great enemy, also known as the Minnesota Golden Gophers.

Basketball

If demographics from the U.S. Census Bureau are to be believed, 86 percent of North Dakota can't jump. This athletic reality makes excelling at basketball a particular challenge.

North Dakotans participate in the annual Fats vs. Thins charity game, today better known as the Fats vs Even Fatters game.

Despite this handicap, basketball remains a state favorite with a rich history. Years ago, intramural leagues would play themed games such as the "fats verses thins," where a dunk involved a donut and Sanka. The games were sponsored by the Jaycees, a group better known today for getting kidnapped and kept for two decades as a sex slave.

Racing

Stock car and other vehicle racing is very popular in North Dakota. Grand Forks, Jamestown, Minot, West Fargo, Rugby and other cities all have small tracks, called "speedways," where local drivers race a variety of cars. Highlights of local track races include "outlaw sprint" series, regional sponsors, and old people yelling into the night abut "that racket."

As with NASCAR, North Dakota car racing origins can be found in the illegal transportation of alcohol. The primary difference in legacies between NASCAR and Dakota racing is that while NASCAR drivers concealed the illicit alcohol in the trunk, Dakota drivers hid it in their bellies.

Tax Dodging

Uses rules similar to dodge ball with stiffer penalties.

Curling

Like most popular state sports, curling involves ice and ridiculous terminology. The sport's aim of throwing "stones" at a "house" should also not be confused with the similar pastime of North Dakotan ne'er-do-wells.

Before crossing a "hog line" a thrower releases a "rock" from the "hack" down the "sheet" while teammates, the third and the skip, join in sweeping the sheet path toward the target, being careful not to "burn" the stone. Sometimes this shot is the hammer.

When a curler yells "die!" at another curler, it is not a wish for death. Usually.

After this photo was taken, these 1930s North Da-
kotan sportsmen let the birds go in the spirit of the
"catch and releae" hunting methods of the period.

Hunting
Yes, you can shoot that.

Cow Tipping
Widely played by Midwesterners in Hollywood movies, cow
tipping is not popular in North Dakota. Other forms of tipping are also not popular in the state.

95

Ice Fishing

A beginning ice fisher will need bait, a sled, set rods, pliers, hooks and line, bucket to sit on, ice pick, schnapps, ice auger, and nothing better to do.

Complaining

Probably the state's second most popular sport. Like soccer in third world countries, complaining is popular because it can be played anywhere with little investment or infrastructure. All one needs is a subject, and an audience. The game is best played with fewer than four participants and is sometimes mixed with hockey as a hybrid pastime.

North Dakota is home to hall of fame complainer Ed Schultz.

Snow Machining

To most North Dakotans, a "snow machine" is a fancy mechanism used by elitists to manufacture snow on hills at which they can then look at from the heated comfort of their lodge. Before "snow machining" was popularized in the American lexicon by an Alaskan man noted for putting lipstick on his pit bull, the sport was known as "snowmobiling."

Allowance: The Property Tax of Parenthood

Fiscal responsibility is a foundation of a North Dakotan's character. Without a solid education in money matters, North Dakota would today be in no better financial straights than the People's Republic of Minnesota to the east.

An essential fiscal education covers the basics of economics and the sharp rhetorical skills an adult North Dakotan will need to complain about federal spending while at the same time living in a tremendous federal welfare state.

A North Dakotan understands that state, federal and international economics work exactly like one's own wallet. If you want something, you have to pay for it by paying cash or taking out a loan. There is nothing more about economics that you need to understand beyond this.

A great way to create North Dakotan fiscal responsibility in your child is with an allowance. But never give a child an allowance for doing nothing. This is called welfare. Ronald Reagan proved welfare didn't work for freedom and liberty against communism in the new morning in America, and it won't work in your home.

Many North Dakotans have declared themselves "right to work families." Indeed, every child has the right to do chores without being forcibly compelled to the standards of his or her siblings.

Some North Dakotan parents like to use a mathematical formula for calculating their child's allowance.

Where X = Dollars (Canadian)

$$X = \frac{\text{per capita North Dakota budget surplus}}{\text{soybean future (\$ per bushel - Oct. delivery)}}$$

Other parents like to use an *à la carte* system where payments are set to corresponding tasks. Other parents use an a la mode system, in which all allowance is paid in ice cream.

Chores and their equivalent U.S. dollar values (good through 2018 or whenever America begins using the UN's New Order Dollar):

- Potato picking - $0.50 / hour
- Beet sugaring - $0.50 / hour
- Taking out the trash - $0.50 / hour
- Taking out the "empties" - $0.50 / hour
- Doing the taxes - $1.50 / hour (Less $1 for every mistake)
- Sandbag filling - $0.75 / hour
- Raking leaves - $0.50 / hour
- Shoveling snow - $1.00 / fallen inch
- Cleaning up the house - $0.30 / hour
- Washing the car - $0.80 / hour
- Working the land- $1.10 / hour
- Working the corner - $12.00 / hour
- Feeding the cat/dog/grandpa - $0.50 / hour
- Babysitting- $0.50 / hour
- "Never ever never letting mommy know." - $10.00 + $2.00 / month
- Outhouse relocation - $3.00 / hour
- Grandma wrangling - $0.65 / hour

NoDaktivity: Why Don't You Go Outside?

Parent-Child Communication:
It's Only Emotion Away

The most effective tool in forming a string bond between you and your child is super glue. The second most effective bonding agent is communication.

A child's brain is like a sponge, pliable and capable of absorbing everything before becoming old, stiff and largely useless. This is why establishing an open channel of communication between parent and child early on is paramount.

While scary in theory, a conversation with your child is actually much easier than it seems. The ways to communicate with your child are numerous and include body language, notes on the refrigerator, and the firm part of the back of your open hand. One form of communication many North Dakotan parents forget to take advantage of is conversation.

But unlike teen pregnancies, conversations don't just happen on their own. Like a fire, a conversation needs a spark. Also like a fire, a parent-child conversation can become an all-destroying conflagration, running amok and scorching all in its path before outside forces can come in and extinguish it. In both cases, a full recovery is rare. So be careful. Below, a few starter questions your child might ask and a few alternative, North Dakotan replies.

Child's Question: What are clouds?
Your Answer: Remember when we talked about Jesus?
Alternative Answer: Go outside.

Child's Question: Why is the flag red, white and blue?
Your Answer: Why don't you love America?
Alternative Answer: Go outside.

Child's Question: Why does the river always flood?
Your Answer: It's God's way of reminding the rest of America we exist, honey.
Alternative Answer: Go outside.

Child's Question: Why are Minnesotans such 'erks?
Your Answer: Jerks, honey, with a "J." Why are Minnesotans suck jerks.
Alternative Answer: Go outside.

Child's Question: Where do babies come from?
Your Answer: Go outside.
Alternative Answer: Go outside.

Sex Ed: It's Not a Pedophile Named Ed
(Probably not but check with your local precinct)

PURSUANT TO BILL ND006-562, THIS CHAPTER HAS BEEN REMOVED FOR FAILURE TO COMPLY WITH THE STATE'S ABSTINENCE-ONLY EDUCATION POLICY.

What are you still doing here?

I thought I told you to go outside.

North Dakotans are incredibly friendly. The reason many North Dakota cities only put a sidewalk on one side of a street is that no pedestrian would ever think to cross a street to avoid another.

Part of the reason for this friendliness is the state's rich cultural tapestry, which in North Dakota literally means stuff held together with tape.

Art

North Dakota's art scene is larger than that of nearly anywhere else in the world. For example, New Salem, ND is home to Salem Sue, the largest roadside dairy cow in the world at 38 feet long and 50 feet tall. At 60 tons, the buffalo statue in Jamestown is the world's largest.

The Louvre may boast Pierre Hebert's "Enfant jouant avec une tortue" (Boy playing with tortoise), but Dunseith has the Wee'l Turtle, made of more than 2,000 tire rims. Meanwhile, Bottineau's collection includes Tommy, the world's largest snowmobile-riding tortoise.

The Whitney collection includes Robert Rauschenberg's "Satellite," a 1955 canvas with oil, fabric, paper and a stuffed pheasant and John Marin's "The Lobster Fisherman." But North Dakota has The Enchanted Highway, a stretch of road from Regent to Galdstone filled with welded metal sculptures, including "Pheasants on the Prairie" and "Fisherman's Dream."

The state is also home to one of the greatest art feuds of all time. While Garrison, Minnesota claims its 15-foot fiberglass Walleye makes it the "Walleye Capital of the World," the art world knows Garrsion, North Dakota's 26-foot fiberglass wall-eye has the last word on the subject.

North Dakota's lesser known Portrait of the Artist's Mother Waiting for Her Son to Call. Also called "Vigbjørn's Mother."

Food

Like to eat? You're going to love being North Dakotan. Love being able to pronounce the name of the food you eat? You might want to try somewhere else, like Ohio.

Just a few of the state's marquee dishes include knoephla, Fleischkuekle, and lutefisk, a delicious fish dish made with lye. Yes, the same stuff the mob uses on corpses in shallow graves. Yum!

North Dakota is also home to dishes that are easy to pronounce, such as mushroom soup casserole, Beetloaf, buttered
buttery butter, Ritz, and the regional favorite, "Heinzburger."

North Dakota offers a number of events for the true gastro-
nomic adventurer.

Sauerkraut Days
Wishek, ND

Rhubarb Festival
Washburn, ND / Grand Forks, ND

Chokecherry Festival
Casselton, ND

Norsk Høstfest
Minot, ND

Drinking

North Dakotans have been known to enjoy an occasional
nightcap, though in the state it is known as a "nighthood."

Known as "America's Siberia," North Dakota regularly finishes
atop lists of the nation's top binge-drinking states, which just
goes to show how government confuses matters. Is it really a
binge if one never stops? Durr.

Film & Television

With sub-zero winters lasting up to six months, North Dakotans have no greater friend than the TV.

North Dakotans did not immediately grasp the concept of how to watch a TV broadcast.

North Dakotans are also intellectually curious and seek out quality films to balance the meat and potatoes that is reality TV.

What film best represents North Dakota? Many would certainly say this honor belongs to "Fargo" simply because that film takes place in the state.

But three years earlier, a far more North Dakotan film was released.

How to Be: NORTH DAKOTA

Starring a young, pre-post-Brad Pitt Jennifer Aniston, 1993's "Leprechaun" told the story of a 600-year-old leprechaun on a murder spree in North Dakota. With lines such as "Don't cut yourself on any of this old rusty metal. If you do, it will make your jaw lock shut," the film became a cult horror classic.

But in North Dakota, Leprechaun was a moving tale about the enduring power of the human spirit. Elderly men across the state sympathized with the plight of a grumpy old immigrant from old Europe who just wanted the youngsters to leave him alone. The leprechaun's madness for gold was seen by other North Dakotans as nothing more than a smart investor who knew gold was a good hedge against ballooning government spending and inflation. The warning about rusty metal and tetanus? Well, damn, that's just common sense.

Also more North Dakotan than "Fargo" is Ingmar Bergman's "The Seventh Seal" and not just because the Cohen brothers are Minneapolis Jews and Bergman was Scandinavian.

"The Seventh Seal" is an unsubtle allegory about what it means to be human. Death himself is a major character, interacting with the protagonist and challenging his belief in life's meaning and his very faith in God. These are sentiments with which anyone who has ever experienced a North Dakotan February is intimately familiar.

The missing "Devils Lake catfish" scene from the Bergman classic.

The state can also be seen in the epic "A Star is Born." This movie tells the tale of a North Dakota farmgirl who runs off to Hollywood to make it big, which she does, but under a different name.

Is there anything more true to the state than North Dakotan youths running away to become somebody else?

Humor
What do North Dakotans do during the summer?
If it happens on a weekend, they go fishing.

A good sense of humor is not only a core North Dakotan characteristic, but also a great coping mechanism. The best

111

antidote to weeks of subzero temperatures is a small home in Florida. The second best is a good laugh... while sitting on the porch of a winter home in Florida.

A Sioux chief unhappy after falling for the first ever boot-black in the telescope gag.

Of course, as with all regions, the state has its own particular brand of humor. Why is it said there is a beautiful woman behind every tree in North Dakota? You just have to be here.

One of the most beloved humor traditions in North Dakota is the "Ole and Lena" joke. The precursor to just about every prime-time sitcom, these jokes center around a dimwitted Scandinavian couple who constantly bicker and rejoice in each other's misfortune. Sheer hilarity.

A few Ole and Lena examples:

After getting married, Ole and Lena are driving down I-94 to honeymoon in Fargo. Halfway there, Ole puts his hand on Lena's knee, to which Lena says, "Oh, Ole, ve're married now. Ya' can go furder." So Ole drove to Minneapolis.

Ole came home from work one day and Lena said, "Remember ve were talking 'bout getting a more expensive apartment?" "Ya," said Ole. "Vell," said Lena, "Ve did. Da landlord just raised da rent!"

Lena found Ole at the outhouse one day. He was throwing dollar bills down the hole. Finally he threw his watch down. "Good grief, vhat ay dooin, Ole?" Lena asked. Ole said, "I dropped two quarters down vere but I'm not goin' down in vhat mess fer just 50 cents."

Like most of North Dakota culture, Ole and Lena jokes represent the peak of the form. Learn to laugh at them and you will learn to laugh with North Dakota.

Religion

North Dakotans are not "Sunday Christians." The state's faithful pay homage to God even on the days when their homes are not nearly underwater.

North Dakota has more churches per capita than any other state. It also claims the highest church-going rates of any state. If you don't believe that, just try to run to the store on a Sunday morning when the in-laws are on their way and you really need to get that vanilla.

If the pie tastes funny, well, that's apparently just His will.

Nodaktivity: Church Service Bingo

"Vikings"	somebody died	"cancer"	snoring
Lord's Prayer	program misspelling	"golf"	bolo tie
"Shhhhhhhhh"	hangover	"In these times..."	sermon prop
Leviticus!	coupon in collection plate	"take a moment"	jogging pants

Holidays, Customs and Udder Stuff

Naugahyde
While its use peaked in the rest of America in the early 1970s, the tanned skin of the wild nauga remains popular in North Dakota.

Bison Vs. Buffalo
Buffalo, home to terrible pro-sports teams, is an industrial wasteland in New York State. A Bison is the mascot of a North Dakota university sports team in the social wasteland of Fargo. Both are delicious in burger form.

"Minnesota Nice"
A more common term for the passive aggressive behavior of the residents to the east, who really deserve credit for doing so well, considering.

Supper
One pea more than "super" is supper! The last *official* meal of the day, supper is what east coast elitists call "dinner."

Sundogs

Also known as a "phantom sun" or a "parhelion." A prairie phenomenon that occurs during sunsets when a bright blaze of light at 22°, the same distance above the horizon as the sun, gives the appearance of a second sun. If you see one, you owe George Lucas royalties.

Sodbuster

Farmers in the late 1800s who moved into the Great Plains to work the pristine expanse of prairie. Their nickname came from the way they busted up the sod to plant crops. Sodbusters shared a name with "union busters," another popular late-1800s vocation.

The Food Security Act of 1985 gave sodbusters a bad name, using the term as the name of a provision that penalized the plowing up of certain grasslands. These lands were named "highly erodible lands" by the US Dept. of Agriculture, leading to government papers with titles like "More HEL is in compliance."

Each summer, Fort Ransom in Ransom County hosts Sodbuster Days. Some North Dakotans still think of themselves as sodbusters, though the stone-sharpening art of flintknapping has fallen off in popularity recently in favor of plain old napping.

Berm

A level, sometimes raised, barrier of grass area between the sidewalk and the road. Yes, you also have to mow that.

Euphorbia esula

Better known as "leafy spurge," or by its scientific name "That Damn Weed that Just Won't Die," euphorbia esulaan is an invasive plant characterized by white milky sap. An invasive immigrant species, leafy spurge moves into an area and takes all of the jobs that would otherwise go to native weeds.

Nodding Donkey

Commonly seen in western North Dakota, a "nodding donkey" is the above ground pumpjack portion of a reciprocating piston pump oil well. This term is derived from the pump's seesawing, in-and-out motion, leading to its other nicknames "grasshopper pump," "thirsty bird" and "Yo' Mamma'"

Some lucky North Dakotans keep nodding donkeys as pets.

In the eastern portion of the state, a "nodding donkey" is an incumbent Democrat.

117

Hotdish

A hotdish is a baked casserole consisting of some kind of meat, some kind of starch, and some vegetable mixed with a canned soup and baked to a golden brown at some kind of temperature. For example, tater tots, hamburger, frozen peas and a can of cream of mushroom soup is a perfect hotdish. The hotdish forms the wide, heavy foundation of the North Dakota food pyramid. Eaten often enough it forms the wide foundation of the heaviest North Dakotans. The hotdish also serves as a peace offering between family members who hate each other.

Alberta Clipper

Sudden, unpredictable burst of harsh weather that comes down from Canada to tear through North Dakotan cities. Not to be confused with "Alberta trippers," a weekend burst of Canadians come down to tear through North Dakotan big box stores. Alberta Clippers are often confused with "Alberta strippers" as both can cause great monetary damage.

Syttende Mai

Also known as Norwegian Constitution Day. May 17 celebrates the day Norway's founding fathers plagiarized the greatest document in the world for their own freedom and liberty and then all shared a hotdish just like a bunch of socialists. In recent years, Syttende Mai has become especially popular with the Scandinavian Tea Party, also known as the Glögg Pärty.

Language and Diction

North Dakotan dialects and vocabulary have evolved over many years to more efficiently communicate region-specific wants and needs.

A few common Dakotaisms:

Acrosst
The proper term for describing a length that was, or will be, crossed.
Sample usage: "We drove from Grand Forks acrosst on Highway 2 to see grampa Minot."

Ahunnerd
One-hundreed
Sample usage: "I've got about ahunnerd empties in my trunk."

Allada
All of the
Sample usage: "Probably take me three days to get allada water out my basement."

Bedderdan
Better than
Sample usage: "They think they're bedderdan us just 'cause they got running water."

Boughted
Purchased
Sample usage: "I don't have registration officer, 'cause I just boughted it off a guy two days ago."

Dares
There is
Sample usage: "Dares something wrong with that boy."

Dees
These
Sample usage: "Dees bars are delicious!"

Dint
Did not
Sample usage: "Owing to a hangover, I dint get out to shovel the walk yet."

Donchaknow
Do you not know? (The "fuggedaboutit" of the Great Plains.)

Gazunteit
God bless you. (For use after sneezing)

120

Hafta
Must do
Sample usage: "I hafta take allada empties out my trunk 'fore I get pulled over."

Djever
Did you ever
Sample usage: "Djever have her bars? Delicious, donchaknow"

Kaaput
It's done.
Sample usage: "That engine's kaaput."

Anudder
Another
Sample usage: "Dis engine's kaaput. Gonna' need anudder."

Yah
Yes; Sure; I agree; Maybe. I'm thinking about it; I'm uncomfortable with your premise but too polite to tell you how wrong you are.
Sample usage: "Yah."

Pritnear
Pretty much
Sample usage: "That engine's pritnear kaaput."

Terdy
Thirty
Sample usage: "Terdy minutes 'till da Vikes game starts."

Terdy-tree
Thirty-three
Sample usage: "Terdy-tree minutes 'till Vikes lose anudder one."

Lent
Loaned; also a Catholic holiday
Sample usage: "I lent him my snow blower."

Oh Fer Cryin Out Loud
Goodness' Sakes
Sample usage: "Oh fer cryin out loud, vill dis vinter never end?"

Uffdah!
This Minnesota term is not used by North Dakotans.

Square Dance!

Like polio and Flag Day, square dancing was largely eradicated in America by the late 20th century. Yet, a healthy number of square dancing groups still operate in the state, where it is the official dance.

American square dancing is derived from the folk dances of numerous immigrant cultures, including those of the British, Caledonians, and Skuares, a forgotten culture known for its inability to make anything but a right turn.

From the beginning, the dance was controversial.

How to Be: NORTH DAKOTA

In 1923, the popularization of the square dance move "Allemande Left," led to harsh punishment by the House Committee on Un-American Activities.

Many religious leaders have forbidden square dancing for its similarity to sex. Sexually transmitted dances are common.

As with many things North Dakotan, the name, "square-dance," wastes nothing. It at once describes the motion through which the dance is performed while at the same time describing the social position of those performing it.

Square dancing is generally made up of movements using an eight count, with each dance consisting of a set of moves for the dancers to follow. Typical square dance choreography is comprised of four parts called A1, A2, B1, and B2. A count is one half of a musical measure, or a quarter note in 2/4 time, also a three-eighth note in 6/8 time. It is also a dude from old Europe who may or may not drink your blood.

The "caller" calls the dance by describing directions to the dancers through coded square dance terms. Typical terms include: allemande; butterfly whirl; do-si-do; promenade: sashay; and ladies chain (not to be confused with Ladies Chain™, a line of pornographic videos).

In some ways, square dance callers are the original free-form rap artists. In almost every other way they are not.

A Guide to the Plains

Some classic examples of calls that would make up a dance:

Allemande left, with the corner maid;
Meet your own and promenade.

Cat in the barn, rat in her mouth
Grab your honey and head her south.

Ambulances and big black hearses;
Swing those doctors; swing those nurses.

Bow to you partner and the corner miss;
To the opposite lady, just blow a kiss.

If you like this book so might your brother;
Then open that wallet and buy a-nother.

NoDaktivity: Landscape Paint by Number

Nothing helps one better appreciate the intricacies of the state's seasons like painting a charming North Dakota landscape. Use the paint-by-numbers color code below, complete a splendid painting of a January North Dakota panorama.

1. blue
3. white
5. brown
7. green
9. purple

2. pink
4. black
6. red
8. yellow
10. orange

The Ballad of Johan Henryson

Some say he's from Farga',
Others say Casselton,
But wrote on the rock in Rugby,
Says he's a Hazen Man.

Henryson he could shovel,
He could push, he could swing,
Went to the sidewalk early mornin'
To hear his shovel ring.

Sven said, "Johan Henryson,
You got a willing spine.
But best lay yer shovel down,
Never'll beat this blower of mine."

A Guide to the Plains

The blower was on the right
Said Johan on the left,
"Fore I let this blower beat me down,
I'll shovel m'self to death."

Johan on the sidewalk,
The snow was it was so high,
Plow went by, tripled the load
Snow almost reached the sky.

Johan Henryson he did shovel,
Through ice, made it sing
But that blower kicked it out
It was the winter king.

Ladies commin' back from church
Saw Johan on one knee,
They all gasped and said,
"We'll put on some coffee."

The shovel that Johan swung,
Old steel, weighed 11 pound.
Heart gave out, spleen did burst
Johan's body hit the ground.

They took Henry out west,
Buried him in Bad Lands.
Every dad now tells his sons
No blower kid, use your hands.

I'm only going to tell you to go outside one more time.

Dying: A North Dakota Way of Life

Facing the prospect of death is never welcome. But a positive attitude can help. For example, don't think about death as the ultimate obliteration of all of your memories and your very consciousness itself, look at it as a chance to get your name in the paper.

North Dakotans recognize human frailty for what it is: a job creator. North Dakota is one of the few states where the obituaries page is still a thriving business for newspapers.

The dying North Dakotan does not leave something as important as an obituary to a stranger such as a newspaper editor or a spouse. So prepare your obituary well ahead of time. Because the final details may be unknown to you now, be as vague as possible and don't forget, this is your last chance to make everyone you knew feel as guilty as possible.

There is a second important detail of dying the North Dakotan way. While a 401(k) or an IRA investment may seem prudent, a true North Dakotan knows the best investment is a gravesite. It's the one piece of property in which your basement will never flood.

Everyone has different opinions about choosing a stone and a site. Be creative. One nice touch is to make sure you buy an adjacent plot for your spouse and have his or her name added to the stone. An extra nice touch is to have the spouse's name and birth date engraved, leaving the date of death to be added later. Nothing will reassure your betrothed more after your passing than constantly seeing his or her own name there next to yours, on a tombstone.

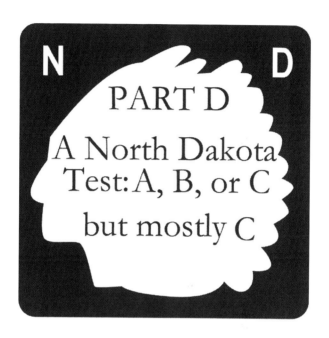

PART D
A North Dakota
Test: A, B, or C
but mostly C

North Dakotans believe in accountability. So based on the No Child Left Behind Act, this book mandates testing to establish higher standards of being North Dakotan.

You have 45 minutes to complete this test. North Dakotans are firm believers in the honor system. (Officials may not be watching, but He is.)

BEGIN TEST NOW

How to Be: NORTH DAKOTA

The town of Rutland cooked and ate the world's largest what?
It weighted 3,591 pounds.
a. "Ziplock" Omelet
b. Squirrel
c. Hamburger

North Dakota's official state beverage is?
a. Schnapps
b. Milk
c. "Potato juice"

North Dakota's State Song features which following line?
a. Is that thine ear below thee boot
b. Black the crude below thee flowing
c. Sweet the winds above thee blowing

Casselton resident Max Taubert built a 50-foot-high pyramid of what? It is believed to be the highest structure of its kind in the world.
a. Hockey pucks
b. Loneliness
c. Oil cans

Turtle Lake is home to a two-ton sculpture of a what?
a. That actor from HBO's "Entourage"
b. A lake
c. A turtle

In 1969, the town of Zap, ND experienced the "Zip to Zap." What was it?
a. A Sesame Street episode Zap's zipper factory
b. A Dr. Suess book about Zap
c. A Spring Break party turned riot that required the National Guard had to subdue.

In 1934, a golfer name George Wegener shot an international hole-in-one as he drove a ball from a tee in Canada into a hole on a green in the United States. What else is George Wegener known for?
a.
b.
c.

All of the below are popular North Dakota yet only one has been deemed "offensive" by national authorities.
a. Lutefisk
b. TruckNutz
c. Fighting Sioux mascot

One of the nation's first mosques was constructed in the town of Ross by Muslim homesteaders. What year was it built?
a. 12 B.C.
b. 9/11
c. 1929

A rare characteristics of the Red River is that it...?
a. Tastes like Kool-Aid
b. Is actually red.
c. Flows north.

An odd state law declares that no establishment can serve a beer in which manner?
a. To a Minnesotan.
b. With a gay lemon wedge.
c. With pretzels.

How to Be: NORTH DAKOTA

What famous product was invented in the state and derives its name from "Dakota?"
a. Skoda automobiles
b. Dakota Fanning
c. Kodak film

When federal troops arrested Indian activist and leader Sitting Bull at Fort Yates, authorities botched the arrest by..."
a. not reading him his Miranda rights.
b. failing to have the proper warrant.
c. shooting him in the head at close range.

There are more registered vehicles in North Dakota than there are...?
a. Unregistered handguns
b. Unregistered laborers
c. Residents

Angie Dickinson was born in North Dakota. She famously appeared in...?
a. Fargo
b. The Janice Dickinson Modeling Agency
c. Rio Bravo

Despite the libertarian, anti-central-government posturing of many of its residents, North Dakota is a federal welfare state, getting back $1.75 for every tax dollar it sends to Washington D.C. Consequently, a North Dakota commemorative quarter (25 cents) is worth:
a. A draft Budweiser (Tuesday night only)
b. 32 cents
c. 25 cents

North Dakota State University's research experiment station in Hettinger is the nation's largest state-owned research center for what kind of mammal?
a. Chupacabras
b. Party Animals
c. Sheep

The image at the left is of:
a.An old woman
b.A young woman
c.Property taxes

The North Dakota sate flag contains the phrase "E Pluribus Unum." How many North Dakota institutes of higher learning offer Latin?
a. 0
b. Zero
c. Nullus

The Bakken formation subsurface of the Williston Basin contains one of the world's most promising oil reserves. How do engineers know which areas of the Bakken source rock are not yet thermally mature?
a. When porosities remain below 5%
b. When permeabilities are under 0.04 millidarcies
c. When it tells them it hates them

How to Be: NORTH DAKOTA

Before George Custer made his last stand, he was stationed at what North Dakota fort?
a. Fort Myers
b. Fortress of Solitude
c. Fort Abraham Lincoln

Mr. Magnusson wants to know, what're you looking at, son?

A: _____
_____
_____
_____

North Dakota is home to several species of snake. Which is the only poisonous one?
a. Cobra
b. Your ex-wife's lawyer
c. Prairie Rattler

President Jefferson was a notorious tax-and-spending pork-barrel socialist. How much of America's money did he piss away to fund Lewis & Clark's pointless "academic" research project?
a. $10 million
b. $3 trillion
c. $2,500

North Dakota is so windy because...
a. Minnesota sucks
b. Montana blows
c. All of the above

CLASSIFIEDS

CALL ME. I want to be part of your dream.

Nobody left in your life who can respond to your deepest desires? Don't suffer alone, call the property tax line.

Call **1-999-PRO-PTAX** and get together with other taxpayers sick of being bilked out of hard earned dollars by an out-of-control local government.

Or, talk with one of our tax professionals, who will slide your appraisal up even while pulling your overall payment down. All in the privacy of your own home. Never attend another school board or municipal council meeting looking for satisfaction ever again. Our operators offer release from the stressful buildup of decades of jacked up rates in return for falling educational standards and local services. But you have to make the first move.

Just $50.00 for the first minute and 0.2% to 4% of the initial charge for every additional minute depending on your area code. For property owners only.

CLASSIFIEDS

Born and raised on a dairy farm in the Midwest, Abe Sauer splits time between North Dakota, Minnesota and Wisconsin. He has written for The Atlantic, Esquire, The Awl, Reuters, Deadspin, The Hairpin, Jest Magazine, and The St. Paul Almanac, amongst others. He is a former senior editor for Fargo's *Casino Enterprise Management Magazine.* He is raising his two daughters to be North Dakotan in spirit.

With love for Angela, Astrid, Frances, Mom and Dad.

For updates, ordering info and more North Dakota humor visit www . BeNorthDakota . com.

Image Credits

Page 16; Institute for Regional Studies, NDSU, Fargo (Folio 102.EnF46.1b)
Page 18; Institute for Regional Studies, NDSU, Fargo (Folio 102EnB45.1c)
Page 20; Library of Congress Prints and Photographs
Page 23; Institute for Regional Studies, NDSU, Fargo (Folio 102.TrR34.1a)
Page 28; Creative Commons (cc-by-sa-2.5)
Page 32; Minneapolis Journal, May 28, 1903, Library of Congress
Page 38; Library of Congress Prints and Photographs Division
Page 41; Library of Congress, Prints & Photographs Division, FSA/OWI
Page 42; Institute for Regional Studies, NDSU, Fargo (Photo Folio 108.5)
Page 44; The Appeal. (Saint Paul, Minn.June 19, 1920; Library of Congress; Minnesota Historical Society; Saint Paul, MN
Page 52-64; Illustrations by Amy Jean Porter; www . amyjeanporter . com
Page 67; Library of Congress Prints and Photographs
Page 69; Barnes County Historical Society (BC22)
Page 75; Library of Congress, Prints & Photographs Division, FSA/OWI
Page 80; Library of Congress, Prints & Photographs Division, FSA/OWI
Page 81; Library of Congress, Prints & Photographs Division, FSA/OWI Collection, [reproduction number, e.g., LC-USF34-9058-C]
Page 89; Warren Sheaf. 1880-current, Library of Congress; Minnesota Historical Society, Saint Paul, MN
Page 90; State Historical Society of North Dakota, William E. (Bill) Shemorry Photograph Collection (1-78H-3)
Page 92; Library of Congress Prints and Photographs
Page 93; State Historical Society of North Dakota, William E. (Bill) Shemorry Photograph Collection (1-20-11-2)
Page 95; Barnes County Historical Society (BC 3-13-1)
Page 100; Library of Congress, Prints & Photographs Division, FSA/OWI
Page 106; Creative Commons (cc-by-sa-2.5); Photo by Bobak Ha'Eri
Page 109; State Historical Society of North Dakota, William E. (Bill) Shemorry Photograph Collection (1-32A-212-10)
Page 110; Svensk Filmindustri (SF); 1957
Page 111; Library of Congress Prints and Photographs
Page 117; by Ian Britton, Creative Commons Attribution-Noncommercial-No Derivative Works 3.0 License
Page 123; Library of Congress, Prints & Photographs Division, FSA/OWI
Page 128; By ND artist JoJo Seames; www .deadsquirrelcomics . com
Page 140; Library of Congress Prints and Photographs Division Wash D.C.
Page 139; Library of Congress; Minnesota Historical Society; Saint Paul, MN
Page 142; Library of Congress; Minnesota Historical Society; Saint Paul, MN

Made in the USA
Lexington, KY
05 January 2012